MEET THE MINIFIGURES

Written by Julia March and Helen Murray

CONTENTS

Hello! Come and meet me and all my friends...

ROCK SINGER

Raise a cheer—and a fist. The Rock Singer has just burst onto the Minifigure scene. Check out their flowing hair, skull T-shirt, and wild makeup. This strutting star is set to dazzle fans' eyes as well as blast their ears. That's rock 'n' roll, baby!

NO WAY!

A rock concert at the V&A Museum in London had to be canceled. Why? Because vibrations from the loud music might have damaged the building.

MINI FACTS

LIKES A crowd full of happy headbanging fans

DISLIKES Crowd-surfing. Too risky!

OFTEN SAYS "Are you ready to rock?"

BAND BACKUP

Rock Singer plays the occasional gig with '80s Musician. He is a great keytar player, but he has to stand behind Rock Singer. There is only one star in this show!

What do rock singers call their breakfast?

Rock-it fuel!

8

HORSE AND GROOM

Horse and Groom are together from morning until it is time to hit the hay. They both love jokes, carrots, and snuggling down to watch TV together. Shows featuring horses are their absolute favorites, of course!

Why couldn't the pony sing in the choir?

Because she was a little horse!

STABLE FRIENDSHIP

Centaur Warrior lives nearby. She often clip-clops in for a natter with Groom. They share an apple or a carrot, and tell each other hay-larious jokes.

 **MINI FACTS**

LIKES Fresh, crunchy carrots

DISLIKES Old, bendy carrots

GREATEST FEAR Developing hay fever. Imagine how annoying that would be!

PUG COSTUME GUY

This canine-costumed Minifigure *really* loves pugs. He likes to wear his special pug costume to put his furry friends at ease. Don't tell Pug Costume Guy, but the pugs actually realized that he wasn't a real dog years ago. Shhh!

What type of dog likes to shower?

A sham**poodle**!

 **MINI FACTS**

LIKES Um, pugs

DISLIKES Misplacing his pug costume

OFTEN SAYS "Good doggo"

NO WAY!

A group of dogs is called a pack, a group of puppies is called a litter... and a group of pugs is called a grumble!

TOP TIP!

Your LEGO® animal can be any color you like—it doesn't have to be realistic.

Large, round eyes

White paws are oval plates

BUILD IT!

Build your favorite animal with LEGO bricks. A perfect pug is Pug Costume Guy's first choice, but his pal Fox Costume Girl has other ideas. When looking for pieces, think about the main features of your animal, such as a floppy tongue, pointy ears, or a waggy tail.

Round tile with eye print

Don't forget a bushy fox tail!

Stacked bricks for legs

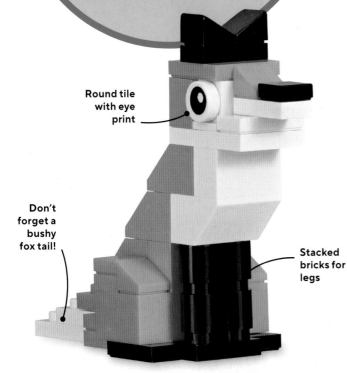

PAWSOME PALS

Fox Costume Girl thinks foxes and chickens are the best animals. Her friend Pug Costume Guy does not agree!

SPACE FAN

5... 4... 3... 2... 1... Blast off! You will usually find Space Fan in a field attempting to get one of her rocket models to take flight. She does not mind if it crashes, though. She enjoys trying to figure out what went wrong!

NO WAY!

A Russian cosmonaut named Yuri Gagarin became the first person in space on April 12, 1961. Sixty years later, tourists are beginning to visit space for the first time!

MINI FACTS

LIKES Calculating rocket trajectories (paths)

DISLIKES Not being able to wear her spaceship T-shirt because it is in the wash

DREAM To launch a LEGO rocket into space

How do you get a baby astronaut to sleep?

Rocket!

COSMIC CHALLENGE

Can you build a rocket at rocket speed? Play with family or friends to see who can build a rocket first in under 60 seconds. Next, give players another 60 seconds to see who can add a launch pad first. Play again by building something new, such as a space buggy, an alien, or a satellite.

HOW TO PLAY

1 Place a big pile of bricks in the middle of everyone and decide what you will build.

2 Set a timer for 60 seconds.

3 The first player to complete their model in under 60 seconds is the winner.

TOP TIP!

Choose something to shout out when you have completed the model, like "Blast off."

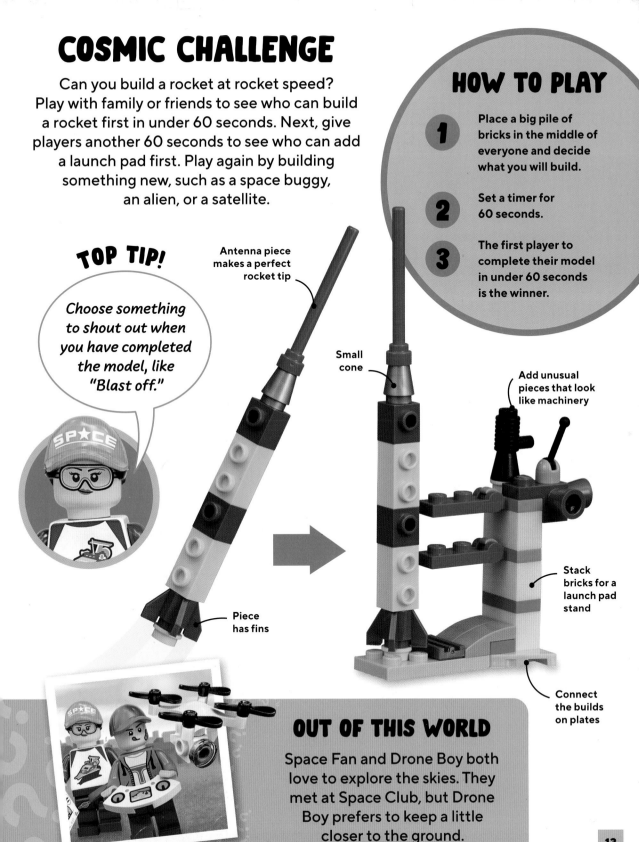

Antenna piece makes a perfect rocket tip

Small cone

Add unusual pieces that look like machinery

Piece has fins

Stack bricks for a launch pad stand

Connect the builds on plates

OUT OF THIS WORLD

Space Fan and Drone Boy both love to explore the skies. They met at Space Club, but Drone Boy prefers to keep a little closer to the ground.

PARTY CLOWN

Why did the clown go to the doctor?

He was feeling funny!

Who can you count on to turn a frown upside down? Party Clown! This cheerful chap never runs out of jokes—or balloons. He keeps a supply of balloons under his hat, ready to be blown up and twisted into funny animal shapes.

 ## MINI FACTS

LIKES The sound of laughter

DISLIKES Balloons that burst at the wrong moment

OFTEN SAYS "Hyuck hyuck!" (That's his laugh!)

PARTY POPPER

Cake Guy is used to giving surprises. He was given one himself when Party Clown popped a balloon behind him as he burst from his cake. What a shock!

NIGHT PROTECTOR

Trusting Night Protector to guard you while you sleep is easy. Visiting her magical castle isn't. It only appears at full moon on the coldest winter night. If you get there, try a slice of her homemade banana bread. It's dreamy!

LIKES The melodious sound of wolves howling

DISLIKES Lunar eclipses when she is expecting visitors

MISSION To watch over people while they sleep

NO WAY!

When you sleep, your brain gives out a chemical that keeps your muscles still. It stops you from acting out any wild, action-packed dreams.

Why should you take a ruler to bed?

To find out how long you sleep!

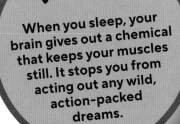

TIME FOR A VISIT

Super Warrior is a time traveler who knows just the right time to travel to Night Protector's castle. Full moon, coldest night, and just as the banana bread is being cut.

BIRDWATCHER

How many birds does it take to change a lightbulb?

Toucan!

Eagle-eyed Birdwatcher travels the world in search of feathered friends to study. A glimpse of a rare one always gets her heart in a flutter. Just give her a pair of binoculars and she is in paradise—even if she doesn't actually spot a bird of paradise!

 **MINI FACTS**

LIKES A refreshing flask of hot tea

DISLIKES Not seeing birds

FAVORITE BIRD Today, the toucan. Tomorrow, who knows?

 **NO WAY!**

A toucan's beak is huge but very light. That is because it is filled with air pockets. Scientists think they help it to stay cool in the tropical forests where it lives.

Short, sharp beak

A jay's tail is blunt and rectangular

TOP TIP!

Tooth plates are great for making beaks, feet, and feathers.

Look for interesting pieces for bird feet, such as robot arms or wrenches

Bill is a yellow tooth plate

Slope for a tufty duck tail

BUILD IT!

Do you love robins? Admire owls? Or is a parrot your pick of the birds? Build your favorites from LEGO pieces. Or, if you prefer, build a bird that exists only in your imagination, like a lesser spotted whistling purple peafowl. Even Birdwatcher won't have seen that one!

Angled piece makes a good parrot beak

This bird is nestled down to sleep

BIRDS OR BEES?

Birdwatcher and Beekeeper both love flying creatures—just not the same kind. Birdwatcher prefers hers a little less likely to sting. Beekeeper prefers his a little less likely to peck.

ROBOT REPAIR TECH

Has your gadget gone wrong? Then call on Robot Repair Tech. This helpful robot can mend a modem or fix a flash drive in no time. It might even change a lightbulb if you ask nicely. That little red bot by its side is its loyal assistant, BD-BD .

NO WAY!

The word "robot" comes from a Czech word meaning "drudgery." Early robots were designed to do jobs too boring or dangerous for humans.

 **MINI FACTS**

LIKES Fixing the unfixable

DISLIKES Having nothing to do

PAYMENT A nice hot cup of engine oil will do

What is a gadget's favorite snack?

Microchips!

WHICH BOT DOES WHAT?

This game is a fun way to test your creativity with your friends. You are each going to create a quirky little robot that does just one particular task. Will yours be Wally the windowbox waterer? Or Valentina the vegetable chopper?

Taps to control water jets

Chainsaw piece

Megaphone for cheerleader bot

Four cones make legs

Antennae can move up or down

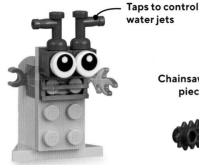

TALKING TECH TOGETHER

Programmer has been hard at work building her own robot. She has made a few little mistakes. Well, nobody's perfect! Robot Repair Tech has helped her put them right.

ALIEN

Wanted: a green alien with two bulbous eyes, wearing an orange suit! This sneaky Minifigure lives their life on the run after stealing an experimental energy crystal from a space lab. Watch out, Alien. The Space Police are after you!

Why did the alien go to the doctor?

They looked a little green!

MINI FACTS

LIKES Stealing crystals

DISLIKES The Space Police

OFTEN SEEN Looking with one bulbous eye over their shoulder to see who is on their trail

IT'S BEHIND YOU!

The Galactic Bounty Hunter did not realize that the Space Police's most-wanted Alien was right behind them! Whoops!

AIRPLANE GIRL

Airplane Girl does not let the small matter of being too young to fly a plane stop her from practicing. She has built her very own plane costume to work on her takeoffs, landings, and in-flight announcements.

What do you call a plane that can't take off?

An error plane!

MINI FACTS

LIKES Eating off a tray with tiny compartments

DISLIKES Bad weather conditions

KNOWN TO BE Accident-prone

NO WAY!

The first-ever powered flight, by the Wright brothers in 1903, covered 120 feet (37 meters). Today, a Boeing 787 can fly 10,000 miles (160,000 kilometers) on a single tank of gas!

FLIGHT CLUB

Rocket Boy and Airplane Girl both dream of taking to the skies when they grow up. For now, they enjoy hanging out in their cool costumes.

DRONE BOY

This Minifigure may be afraid of heights, but he has found a safe way to explore the skies. Drone Boy's awesome drone allows him to discover unexplored places. He uses its camera to take amazing photographs from way up high.

How did the storekeeper realize that drones were so popular?

They were flying off the shelves!

MINI FACTS

LIKES Visiting new places

DISLIKES Getting knocked by his drone

BEST MOMENT Winning a "most llamas in a photo" prize in his local newspaper

Rotor blade

Cable for pulling up passengers

BUILD IT!

Drone Boy's drone sometimes gets a bit too close to flying vehicles. What might he have seen in the sky? Why not try building some flying LEGO vehicles, such as a helicopter or a plane, or build your own LEGO drone. Look for pieces in your collection that would make good propellers and wings.

Propeller is a dish piece

This seaplane has a float for landing on water

A drone can be made with just a handful of pieces

DRONE HERO

Drone Boy was exploring a beach when he discovered Shipwreck Survivor! The scruffy Minifigure made it clear that he did not want to be rescued, though!

23

GARDENER

This green-fingered Minifigure loves tending to her glorious garden. She is happiest when she can share her beautiful blooms and homegrown fruit and vegetables with her family and friends.

What did the tree wear to the pool party?

Swimming trunks!

MINI FACTS

LIKES Being surrounded by family, friends, and plants

DISLIKES Slugs eating her plants

FAVORITE GARDEN DECORATION Pink flamingo

BLOOMING FRIENDSHIP

Flowerpot Girl and Gardener were destined to be friends. They both like to chat— especially about flowers!

VIOLIN KID

Fiddle me this! Do you think there is a song that Violin Kid can't play? No, this musical Minifigure can play anything! He is a popular party guest. Everyone wants him to play their favorite song.

MINI FACTS

LIKES Learning new songs

DISLIKES Strings breaking on his violin

MUSICAL STYLE Classical, rock, country fiddle... everything!

NO WAY!

The violin was invented in Italy in the 1500s—more than 500 years ago. It belongs to the stringed family of instruments.

Why did the musician climb the ladder?

To reach the high notes!

TAKE A BOW

Violin Kid enjoys all kinds of music. He is trained in classical music, but he likes to rock out with his pal Rock Singer on stage.

WE LOVE COSTUMES!

Minifigures adore dressing up—whether there is a party or not! You will find Minifigures dressed as animals, plants, foods, and even LEGO bricks. Which is your favorite Minifigure costume?

Pick me! I must be your favorite!

I think you'll agree that my costume is pawsome!

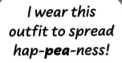

CAT COSTUME GIRL

What do cats eat for breakfast?

Mice crispies!

This Minifigure likes to party! She climbs on furniture and knocks things off tables, but nobody seems to mind. When the excitement gets too much, she finds a sunny spot for a nap. Purr-fect!

NO WAY!

Zzzz... Cats spend around two-thirds of their lives sleeping! But even when they are asleep, their senses remain alert.

MINI FACTS

LIKES Chasing mice

DISLIKES Running out of treats

FAVORITE PARTY ACTIVITY Pouncing on balloons

CATASTROPHE

Cat Costume Girl once helped Dog Sitter take care of some dogs. It was a very tiring day because the dogs just wanted to chase her!

JUNGLE EXPLORER

The legendary Jungle Explorer has adventured to places few Minifigures have seen. He has spotted dinosaurs and yeti, but will he find the brickmeleon, the rarest and most color-changing lizard in the world?

MINI FACTS

LIKES Voyaging far from home

DISLIKES Rolling up his sleeping bag

OCCASIONALLY FOUND At the movie theater, watching one of the movies based on his adventures

What is the biggest ant in the world?

An eleph-ant!

GLOBETROTTERS

Jungle Explorer spotted a rare sighting in South America: Birdwatcher! They chatted about their trips.

FOREST ELF

If you go down to the woods today, you might catch a glimpse of Forest Elf. Ask him to grant you a wish, but be quick or he will scamper away into the ferns. All you will hear is "tee hee hee!" coming from behind a toadstool. But which one?

What kind of photographs do elves like best?

Elfies!

NO WAY!

In 1917, two girls from Yorkshire, UK, photographed cutouts of elves and fairies. They claimed the little creatures were real—and many adults believed them.

MINI FACTS

LIKES Frolicking

DISLIKES Losing his acorn hat in the undergrowth

FAVORITE GAME Hide -and-seek

TOP TIP!

Be adventurous. This is a magical place, so trees could be blue and toadstools silver.

BUILD IT!

Elves are magical, so they need a magical home. Build an enchanted forest with lots of places for them to hide out. Curly plants, toadstools, and clumps of flowers are good for creating a dense undergrowth. Why not give your trees eyes and mouths? They could be the Forest Elf's lookouts, shouting a warning when they see someone coming.

Attach leaf pieces at different heights

Look for plant pieces in your collection

Cone piece for toadstool stalk

WHAT IS YOUR WISH?

Airplane Girl's biggest wish is to become a pilot one day. Forest Elf says she can be anything she wants. She just has to believe in her elf!

RACE CAR GUY

Why did the car get a puncture?

There was a fork in the road!

Vroom vroom! Race Car Guy whizzes everywhere at top speed, usually making loud engine noises. Where is he going? Wherever it is, he wants to get there fast, fast, fast. You could say he lives life in the fast lane.

MINI FACTS

LIKES Getting to the party before anyone else

DISLIKES Being overtaken. Not that anyone's done it!

FAVOURITE MEAL Spaghetti car-bonara

FAST FRIENDS

Race Car Guy and Mountain Biker often go for a spin together. He relies on his fast feet while she prefers pedal power.

Can you feel the next piece you need in the bag?

Before the start, each player gets a set of wheels

CAR RACE

This game is a special kind of car race. Players compete to finish a car build first. But they might hit a roadblock—they need to pick the correct piece from the bag. Who will be first to the finish line?

HOW TO PLAY

1 Build a simple car. This will be the car that everyone will try to copy, so you will need to make sure you have multiples of the same pieces. Place this car model on the table for everyone to see.

2 If you have three players, for example, place three sets of the bricks needed to build the car into a bag. This is the brick selector bag.

3 Players take turns to pull a brick from the bag (with eyes closed!), and gradually build their car.

4 If a player pulls out a brick they don't need, they must put it back and try again in the next round. The first player to complete their car is the winner!

A steering wheel is given to each player

Yes! I've got this piece at last!

Too late... I've finished mine. Toot toot!

1x4 tile with studs

BREAKDANCER

Hey, check out this Minifigure's moves! She kicks, she drops, she spins, and she freezes. Wherever Breakdancer goes, her brickbeats go with her, so never ask her to turn off her boombox and sit down. She might just flip!

NO WAY!

In 2024, "breaking" will become an Olympic sport for the first time. It has come a long way since its beginnings on the streets of New York in the early 1970s.

MINI FACTS

LIKES The urban lifestyle

DISLIKES Snapping a lace on a shoe. Snapping both laces is even worse!

SIGNATURE MOVE "The Brick"

Why do dogs make bad dancers?

They have two left feet!

BUSTING MOVES

Party Clown went to watch his friend Breakdancer in a contest. She said there would be lots of popping, so he took plenty of balloons.

SHOWER GUY

"La la la la la..." Every morning, Shower Guy belts out his favorite songs as he scrubs away happily with his loofah. The bathroom acoustics really give his voice that extra something. What will it be today? Opera, pop, or rub-a-dub?

> Who stole the Minifigure's soap?
>
> A robber duck!

MINI FACTS

LIKES His rubber duck, Quackers

DISLIKES Running out of shower gel... eek!

OFTEN SAYS There's no place like foam!

DUETTING DUO

Shower Guy was nervous when Cabaret Singer invited him to her club for a duet. To make himself feel at home, he rocked up in his towel and shower cap.

ELEPHANT COSTUME GIRL

What do you call an elephant that won't take a bath?

*A **smellyphant!***

Real elephants can't dance, but Elephant Costume Girl certainly can. She is dainty and light on her feet, just like the mouse that has given her a shock by jumping onto her hand. It probably just wants to dance to some trumpet music with her!

NO WAY!

Elephants might not be good dancers, but they are great swimmers. They can even swim underwater. How do they breathe? They use their trunks as snorkels!

MINI FACTS

LIKES Peanuts, peanuts, peanuts!

DISLIKES Getting her tutu in a twist

OFTEN SEEN Practicing her pirouettes and pliés

TOP TIP!

Study pictures of real animals to help you get the details right.

Flowers make the tufts on the horns

BUILD IT!

Be like Elephant Costume Girl—she never forgets the details. Have you noticed how an elephant's trunk flares out at the tip? Or that giraffes have little tufts on their horns? Use LEGO® bricks to build some animals with these special little details. They can really add personality!

Giraffes have a pattern of big, patchy spots

ANIMAL SPOTTERS

Ladybug Girl often spots one of her favorite creatures in the local park. Elephant Costume Girl hasn't been so lucky. Maybe one day!

Big forehead is curved slopes

Closed eye and droopy ear show elephant is relaxed

Plate with long bar is a tusk

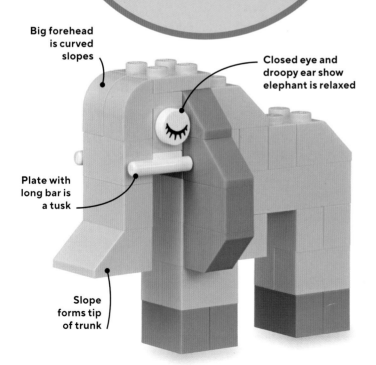

Slope forms tip of trunk

ATHLETE

It can be hard to keep track of Athlete's favorite sport—because she likes them all! Today, she might be throwing the discus or javelin, but tomorrow she could be running a marathon or taking part in a cycling race. Watch this Minifigure go!

What's an insect's favorite sport?

Cricket!

NO WAY!

Athlete Jan Železný holds the world record for throwing the javelin 323 feet (98.48 meters). This is almost the same length as a soccer pitch!

MINI FACTS

LIKES Keeping fit

DISLIKES Losing

FAVORITE PLACE The room where she keeps her many, many medals

READY, SET, LET GO!

Athlete challenges you to practice throwing with this LEGO brick toss game. Build a frame and see how many points you and your friends can score with 10 bricks each. Stand behind a toss line and carefully throw your bricks into the frame. Landing in the central ring will earn you the most points!

HOW TO PLAY

1 Build a frame with three rings inside. The smaller the ring, the more points you will score.

2 Place the board on a flat surface and take five steps back. Mark the toss line with a brick to make sure everyone stands in the same place when they throw.

3 Everyone gets 10 small bricks to throw into the frame. The person with the highest total score wins!

Score 10 points when a brick lands in the center

Landing in the outside ring earns you one point

Wall is one brick high

Bricks tossed in the middle ring earn five points

32x32 plate

GOOD SPORT

It is not hard to see which of these sporty Minifigures takes their training the most seriously. Athlete finds it strange that Martial Arts Boy is not interested in winning at all!

39

VIDEO GAME CHAMP

What happened when the Minifigure's gaming device crashed?

*He was in-**console**-able!*

Video Game Champ is the king of the console. Just ask his army of online fans who hang on to his every word while watching him in action. He always takes it to the next level!

MINI FACTS

LIKES Topping the leaderboards

DISLIKES Waiting too long for a new LEGO video game

OFTEN SAYS "Game over, man!"

PLAY-BOX

SPACE GAME

A BOT AS A BUDDY

Video Game Champ loves putting his gadgets through their paces, and Robot Repair Tech is a bot who loves fixing them. They have found the perfect platform for friendship.

Ouch! Cactus Girl thinks she may have made a mistake with her party costume. She loves hugging her friends, but her prickly costume might jab them. And how will she pick up cake? At least she will have the dance floor all to herself!

 MINI FACTS

LIKES Cake (if she can find someone to feed it to her)

DISLIKES Being mistaken for a pickle

HOBBY She *used* to like making balloon animals

What did the happy cactus say to the grumpy cactus?

You're a bit prickly!

SPIKY AND SPICY

Chili Costume Fan is happy to help Cactus Girl drink some milk. She always has some on hand in case the hot food she loves is just a bit *too* spicy.

NO WAY!

Some cacti can go for up to two years without water! They are adapted to life in deserts and other dry places where it hardly ever rains.

CAKE GUY

MINI FACTS

LIKES Birthdays, weddings, anniversaries...

DISLIKES Thick icing that hurts your head when you break through it

OFTEN SAYS "SURPRISE!"

What a surprise! The Minifigures were about to tuck into a delicious looking cake when out popped Cake Guy, waving and grinning. The cake is wrecked and no one can eat it now, but who wouldn't forgive him? He's just so sweet!

What's the best thing to put into a cake?

Your teeth!

NO WAY!

The oldest cake in the world is on display at a museum in Switzerland. It comes from ancient Egypt, and was baked more than 4,000 years ago.

TEAM BAKE

Rugby Player is a keen baker. Whipping up a batch of cupcakes is his favorite off-pitch activity. His pal Cake Guy says they are yummy!

BUILD IT!

Who wants some LEGO cake? Why not build a big celebration cake, like the one Cake Guy jumped out of? You could have one, two, or even three tiers. Then add candles, swirls, flowers, or anything you fancy. Don't forget to make some little cupcakes, too. They will keep Rugby Player happy!

A flame piece tops the candle

Pink icing swirls

Different colors for different cake layers

Domed red brick makes a maraschino cherry

Icing can be any color plates

Round plates as sugar sprinkles

Eyes come in different colors

TOP TIP!

Adding eyes or other features makes cupcakes look really cute.

DOG SITTER

PACK OF TWO

Pug Costume Guy is Dog Sitter's best buddy. She wishes he would put that bone down, though. She wants to teach him to fetch some cookies.

Time for walkies! Dog Sitter strolls through the park every day, surrounded by her happy canine crew. The smile only leaves her face when she has to stop for a moment and scoop. What *are* they feeding that dachshund?

What's a dog's favorite pizza?

Pupperoni!

MINI FACTS

LIKES Throwing sticks and having them brought back to her

DISLIKES Scooping. Oh well, it has to be done!

LITTLE KNOWN SKILL Pawtrait painting

SUPER WARRIOR

This time traveler battles nobly to save... themself. Super Warrior is back to warn their younger, lazier, greedier self of the mistakes they are about to make. Or maybe to have fun making them all over again.

NO WAY!

When we look up at the night sky we are looking back in time. It takes years for light from stars to travel through space, so we see them as they were long ago.

Have I told you about my time traveler friends?

We go back years!

NO DRAMA!

Even time travelers need a little time out. Super Warrior feels super chill when hanging out with Llama Costume Girl on her ranch.

THAT'S ENTERTAINMENT!

These Minifigures are a talented bunch! Watch them bust some awesome dance moves. Listen to them sing and play beautiful music. Or laugh at their silly jokes! Which Minifigure would you like to entertain you?

What happens when a clown retires?

They leave big shoes to fill!

LA LA LAA! If I sing loudly enough, nobody will notice I can't play this.
LAAAAAAAAH! Everyone, follow my lead!

RUGBY PLAYER

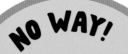
Which Minifigure is ready to try, try, and try again? It's Rugby Player! This sports hero never stops. When he isn't scoring tries and nailing drop goals, he is perfecting tasty new cupcake toppings.

 **MINI FACTS**

LIKES Winning the ball in a scrum

DISLIKES His team losing a match. Boo!

SKILL Baking cupcakes. Mmm... cupcakes!

SPORTS TALK

Rugby Player and Athlete struck up a friendship at the gym. Now they meet often to share the latest sports news (and maybe a cupcake or two).

Why did Cinderella get kicked off the rugby team?

Because she kept running away from the ball!

VIKING

Forget raiding—Viking would rather be reading. He is a stay-at-home scholar who prefers family and farm to fighting. But don't ask him why there are no horns on his helmet. He will tell you to go and read a good history book.

MINI FACTS

LIKES A nice hot, steamy bath

DISLIKES When his longboat springs a leak

HOBBIES Skiing and jewelery making

How do Vikings send long-distance messages?

In Norse code!

FIGHT CLUB

Viking knows he really might have to fight one day. He sharpens his skills during sparring sessions with his spooky friend Fright Knight.

FIREFIGHTER

Where's the fire? Firefighter lets everyone know, and loudly. Through her shiny megaphone, she directs her team with cool authority. Firefighter is the one to trust when things are heating up.

NO WAY!

When a call to a fire comes in, a firefighter must be ready as quickly as they can. The world record for dressing a firefighter is just over 27 seconds!

What did the flame say when he fell in love?

I found my perfect match!

MINI FACTS

LIKES Carving sculptures out of ice

DISLIKES Extra chili on her pizza

DREAM To retire to an ice house in Antarctica

BUILD IT!

In most countries of the world, fire engines are bright red. Nobody is sure why, but Firefighter thinks it might be because red looks so fiery. See how many red bricks you have in your collection. You can build a simple fire engine out of just a handful of bricks.

TOP TIP!

Don't limit yourself to four wheels. Some fire engines have up to eight!

Ladder moves on a plate with clip

Blue and red emergency lights

Tiny wheels made from round plates

EMERGENCY SERVICES UNITE!

"Officer, there's a fire!" At Firefighter's alert, 1978 Police Officer begins directing traffic away from the area. He knows the drill. He has been doing his job for more than 40 years.

BIRTHDAY PARTY GIRL

Birthday Party Girl will never forget 2018. She was invited to her very first LEGO party—a celebration of 40 years of Minifigure fun. Did she enjoy it? Absolutely! She told everyone it was the best party she had ever been to.

MINI FACTS

LIKES Presents, games, balloons, and silly hats

DISLIKES Going home when the party is over

FAVORITE SONG "Happy Birthday to You"

> What does everyone get on their birthday?
>
> A year older!

NO WAY!

The record for most candles on a birthday cake is 72,585. The cake was 80.5 feet (24.5 meters) long and it took 100 people to make it.

MINGLING MINIFIGURES

The friendly Minifigures love to mingle at parties, but having their parts mixed up is taking things a bit far. In this game, you have to put them together without looking. Here is a tip: have a good feel of your Minifigures and their accessories before you begin.

HOW TO PLAY

1 Pick six to eight Minifigures. Pull them apart and mix up the pieces with your hands.

2 Wearing a blindfold, try to put the Minifigures back together. No peeking!

3 When you're done, take off the blindfold. Did you get it right, or is there a Minifigure mix-up in front of you?

Hey! Who's got my rubber duck?

NEWBIE PAIR

Birthday Party Girl went to her first party with another newbie—Birthday Party Boy. They still look for each other at parties and other celebrations.

CABARET SINGER

Why did the singer get locked out of her apartment?

She couldn't find the right key!

Cabaret Singer just loves to be in the spotlight. Every night, she takes the stage at the Brick and Anchor Club, belting out a medley of LEGO songs. This delightful diva has the audience spellbound—and she knows it!

MINI FACTS

LIKES Wearing extravagant costumes

DISLIKES When her microphone cuts out mid-performance

OFTEN SAYS "Laaaaaaaah!"

SWEET HARMONY

Their musical tastes differ, but Cabaret Singer and Breakdancer have one thing in common. When they hear the first beats of a song, they jump to their feet.

GALACTIC BOUNTY HUNTER

Space fugitives beware—Galactic Bounty Hunter could be on your tail. This cunning alien chases the riskiest, richest bounties, and won't stop until they get them. How do they find their targets? With the help of holographic wanted posters.

NO WAY!

In some US states, bounty hunting is a real job. Bounty hunters make a living by catching people who have failed to appear in court and have gone on the run.

MINI FACTS

LIKES Risks and rewards

DISLIKES Being tickled. Please, just don't!

ORIGIN A remote star system. They won't say more... that might spoil the mystery

What did the bounty hunter say when they caught the alien herb thief?

"It was only a matter of thyme!"

WANTED: GALACTIC FRIENDS

Space Creature was once a criminal hunted all over the galaxy. Now the alien has given up crime, they are off Bounty Hunter's target list—and on their friend list instead!

WANTED
BUILT OR BROKEN
REWARD
#300,000,000

UNICORN GUY

What happened when the wizard was really naughty at school?

*He got ex-**spelled**!*

Unicorn Guy brings a little magic to every party. Wizards, elves, treasure, and mythical beasts galore feature in all his games. If only he could magic up a way to stop his horn getting stuck in everything around him!

MINI FACTS

LIKES Changing game rules... as if by magic

DISLIKES Getting woolly sweaters tangled on his pointy horn

DREAM HOME A fairy-tale castle with gold turrets

NO WAY!

In medieval times, people believed unicorns had healing powers. Some rich people were fooled into buying walrus tusks, thinking they were unicorn horns.

BUILD IT!

We all know what a unicorn looks like. It's a horse with a horn, right? Well, Unicorn Guy wants to remind you that your unicorn can have any other features you want. Wings? Why not? Six legs? For sure! As for color, there is a whole magical rainbow of LEGO bricks to choose from.

Horn can be any color

Big eyes create a really cute look

Wings turn a unicorn into an alicorn

Round bricks make good legs

Tail made from slope pieces

TOP TIP!

If you don't have a horn piece, just use a cone or a bar.

FOREST FROLICKS

Forest Elf and Unicorn Guy love a game of hide-and-seek in the woods. Unicorn Guy usually wins. Forest Elf gives away his hiding place with a "tee hee hee!".

PIRATE GIRL

Ahoy there! Meet Pirate Girl. She sails the seven seas aboard her schooner, the *Anne Bonny*. Has she found any buried treasure? Yes, but she won't say where it is. Maybe she is keeping it under her hat.

What is a pirate's favorite letter?

RRRRRR!

NO WAY!

Anne Bonny was a real pirate in the 1700s. Anne's successful raids were legendary. Many believed the superstition that a woman on a ship brought bad luck. She proved them wrong!

MINI FACTS

LIKES The LEGO ship in a bottle she built by herself

DISLIKES Swabbing the deck

OFTEN SAYS "Yo-ho-ho and a bottle of fizzy orange!"

SHIPWRECK GAME

Forget pieces of eight—for this game, you only need 20 LEGO pieces. The aim is to build a series of models using one brick fewer each time. Start with a ship, then break it up to create different builds. You don't have to keep up the pirate theme, but you must throw one piece overboard before each new build.

HOW TO PLAY

1 Choose 20 LEGO elements. They should be a range of different shapes and sizes.

2 Using all 20 pieces, build a jolly pirate ship. Now wreck it! When the ship is in bits, take one piece away and make a new build with the 19 pieces remaining.

3 Every time you finish a model, take another piece away. Try to keep going until there is just one brick left.

Wedge plate looks like a sail

Flame pieces as water jets

Plates are useful to keep

Ship's cannons are now elephant ears

Trunk is a plate with bar

Slope forms the head of the hammer

Could this be the final piece?

CREW OF TWO

Viking and Pirate Girl sometimes get together to sing sea shanties on the beach. She sings high and he sings low, but they both sing with a yo-ho-ho!

59

MARTIAL ARTS BOY

Martial Arts Boy has spent hours training in the dojo. He has been learning a new skill with his nunchaku—the Helicopter Spin. Now he has finally cracked it! Time to head home and use his new skill to crack some walnuts in front of the TV.

What martial art are bakers experts in?

Tae kwon dough!

MARTIAL MATES

White suit or jaguar-spotted armor? Martial Arts Boy and Ancient Warrior do not agree on who is best dressed. But they do agree not to fight over it.

FOX COSTUME GIRL

This Minifigure sneaks around farms, peeking into henhouses. Fox Costume Girl is eager to bag herself a chicken, but it isn't dinner she is craving. She is a strict vegetarian who just wants a big, warm, feathery pet to look after.

NO WAY!

Foxes are part of the dog family, but their climbing skills are more like a cat's. A fox can easily climb a 6 foot (1.8 meter) fence. Some of them even go up trees!

MINI FACTS

LIKES Country walks

DISLIKES Getting pecked while trying to catch a chicken

OFTEN SAYS "Here, chickie, chickie..."

Why did the chicken cross the soccer pitch?

Because the referee called "fowl"!

BEAR HUGS

Fox Costume Girl can't bear it if a catch gets away! Never mind. She will feel better after a rainbow-colored hug from Bear Costume Guy.

SEA RESCUER

Sea Rescuer has a deep love for sea turtles. She will go to the deepest levels of the ocean to prove it, too. If she finds a sick or injured turtle, she tenderly nurses it back to health. These animals are endangered, so every one of them is precious.

Why do turtles never forget?

They have turtle recall!

MINI FACTS

LIKES Collecting treasure. Pirate Queen's mug counts as treasure, right?

DISLIKES Finding litter in the sea

BEST MOMENT Releasing a turtle back into the ocean after its injuries have healed

NO WAY!

Turtles can stay underwater for up to five hours before coming up for air. How? They conserve oxygen by slowing their heart to one beat every few minutes.

Large eyes give an alert look

Slopes form octopus's bulbous head

BUILD IT!

Sea animals come in all shapes and sizes. Just ask Sea Rescuer. She discovers all kinds of underwater creatures on her adventures. As well as fish, there are octopuses, worms, sea urchins, crabs, whales, clams, and even snakes under the sea. Find your most unusual LEGO pieces and see what you can make with them.

Eight stable legs to stand on

Curved slopes for fins

TOP TIP!

Use leafy LEGO elements to build a seaweed world for your animals.

Clownfish have orange faces

TEAM UP FOR THE TURTLES

"Stay off the beach, people. Turtles hatching!" Sea Rescuer is glad Firefighter is around. Her megaphone is perfect for warning people to give the baby turtles some room.

PIÑATA BOY

Nobody loves a birthday party more than Piñata Boy. If there is a celebration going on, he will be there, pronto. And as soon as he gets a chance, he will bash that papier-mâché animal until the candy comes tumbling out. Viva la piñata!

MINI FACTS

LIKES Party invitations

DISLIKES Someone else having the first try

DREAM To find a piñata filled with LEGO bricks instead of candy

NO WAY!

In Mexico, there are shops that sell only piñatas. They come shaped like animals, stars, rockets, superheroes, or even unpopular politicians!

What happened when the Minifigure went for the piñata-breaking record?

He smashed it!

PICK A BUILD IDEA FROM A HAT

Piñata Boy thinks piñatas are the best party activity, but he does know a fun LEGO building game, too. All you need is a pile of LEGO bricks, paper, a pen, and a hat. Your hat doesn't have to be a sombrero like Piñata Boy's—any will do!

HOW TO PLAY

1 Grab a pile of LEGO bricks of different shapes and colors. Now grab some friends.

2 Ask everyone to write three building ideas on separate pieces of paper, and fold them up. Then put the ideas into a hat. If you don't have a hat, just use a bag.

3 Each player pulls out an idea. Set a timer for five minutes and all begin building. Can you guess what everyone has built?

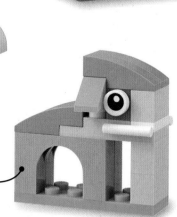

Slope pieces for roof

Yellow bricks with eyes

Elephant legs formed by arch bricks

Plate with handles as antennae

POPULAR PARTYGOERS

Firework Guy and Piñata Boy are fun guests at any Minifigure celebration. They make sure the party goes with a bang and everyone has a smashing time.

OUT OF THIS WORLD!

Some Minifigures come all the way from outer space. Others come from distant magical lands. And some only appear if you are very lucky—or unlucky! Which of these mysterious Minifigures would you like to bump into?

It's nice to get away from the snow for a while.

I am no ordinary monkey!

MUMMY QUEEN

NO WAY!

Ancient Egyptians didn't use money. The workers who built the pyramids were paid in beer and bread instead. It was quite a popular job!

Mummy Queen once lived in a palace in ancient Egypt. Today, her home is a pyramid. Her servants are gone, so she makes her own tea now. But that's fine. She is happy unwinding with her scorpion, scarab, and spider friends.

MINI FACTS

LIKES Flamboyant jewelery. Real gold, of course!

DISLIKES Constantly sweeping up sand

OFTEN SAYS "Mummy knows best!"

What kind of music do mummies love?

Wrap!

ROYAL TEA

Mummy Queen loves having Monkey King over for tea. He likes it strong with a drop of honey. But please—no sand in the bottom of the cup!

TROUBADOUR

Throw him a coin or two and Troubadour will play you a tune on his lute. This traveling minstrel isn't too good at playing it, but don't try asking for your money back. He will probably reply with a cheery "Hey nonny... NO!"

Why did the the minstrel get in trouble?

He was luting in the street!

MINI FACTS

LIKES Colorful clothing

DISLIKES People who stick their fingers in their ears. Why would they do that?

HOME None—he is always on the road

WHAT A RACKET!

Shower Guy foolishly asked Troubadour to play him a tune. It was so off-key he had to pull his shower cap over his ears to shut it out.

PEAPOD COSTUME GIRL

Peapod Costume Girl would spend all day in the garden if she could. She hopes to one day meet someone who loves gardening and vegetable costumes as much as she does. She is sure they would get on like two peas in a pod.

What is the fastest vegetable?

A runner bean!

 **MINI FACTS**

LIKES Growing and cooking vegetables

DISLIKES Getting holes in the knees of her costumes

FAVORITE VEGETABLE Peas, carrots, zucchini... How can anyone choose just one?

NO WAY!

Potatoes were the first food to be grown in space. In 1995, potato plants were taken into space on the *Columbia* space shuttle to see if they could be grown. They could!

Leaves are attached slightly away from the corn

BUILD IT!

Peapod Costume Girl loves to grow lots of different fruits and vegetables in her garden. What fruits and vegetables can you build with your LEGO® collection? Lots of orange bricks? Why not try carrots? Yellow bricks? How about sweet corn? Let the colors of your bricks inspire you. Plant and leaf pieces are useful, too!

Tiny plates look like apple seeds

Green top makes carrot look freshly picked

Leaf pieces for broccoli head

WE DIG VEGETABLES

Peapod Costume Girl has loved gardening since her grandma, Gardener, taught her as a young girl. They grow all kinds of delicious vegetables together.

BRICK COSTUME GUY

Brick Costume Guy knows everything there is to know about LEGO bricks and minifigures. He was pumped to celebrate the 10th anniversary of the LEGO® Minifigures series in 2020.

What did the LEGO aliens say when they landed on Earth?

We come in pieces!

MINI FACTS

LIKES Tearing into a LEGO Minifigures bag to see who is inside

DISLIKES Stepping on LEGO bricks with bare feet

FAVORITE MINIFIGURE 1978 Police Officer

SAME-BRICK CHALLENGE

Give making models with bricks that are all the same size a try. Sort your elements into piles by type, such as 1x2 bricks and 1x4 plates, and choose a type of piece to build with. These models are all made from 1x2 bricks. What can you build using just one kind of brick?

HOW TO PLAY

1 Sort your elements into piles by type.

2 Choose one size of brick to build with. The bricks need to be the same size and shape, but can be any color.

3 See how many models you can build. Will your friends and family be able to guess what you've made?

Lighter yellow bricks look like spots

A transparent brick makes an eye for the whale

Stacked bricks form this snail's shell

Snail's shell stands out in blue

BRICK BEST BUDDIES

These Minifigures have built a beautiful friendship over their shared love of LEGO bricks. Their brick costumes even attach to other LEGO bricks.

1978 POLICE OFFICER

This hardworking Minifigure was based on the first-ever LEGO minifigure, created more than 40 years ago! He is even carrying a mini version of the set that he originally came with. He looks happy now, but he could not fit inside his first little police car!

MINI FACTS

LIKES Serving his community

DISLIKES Having to learn to use new technology

UPDATED WITH A printed torso—he used to have a sticker on his chest

What did the policeman say to his tummy?

You're under a vest!

SPACE CADET

Space Police Guy visited 1978 Police Officer for training. He was taught about patrolling the streets with a smile... although it took him a while to learn!

ANCIENT WARRIOR

Ancient Warrior has dedicated his life to tracking down the jaguar. The rare spotted cat has proved very hard to find. Ancient Warrior does not mind too much. He is immensely proud of his spotted outfit, which he made from scratch.

Why did the jaguar stop playing cards?

Because all the other players were cheetahs!

WANDERING WARRIOR

Mummy Queen was excited to have a visit from Ancient Warrior. Very few Minifigures travel to her pyramid.

LADYBUG GIRL

Why don't ladybugs like playing hide-and-seek?

They always get spotted!

Once upon a time, there was an ordinary ladybug who was transformed by a mean wizard during a duel. Only an enchanted leaf can return her to her true form. Well... actually, she is just a girl in a ladybug costume who likes making up stories!

MINI FACTS

LIKES Reading, writing, and telling stories

DISLIKES Getting writer's block

OFTEN FOUND At the library

STORY TIME

Ladybug Girl's stories are full of amazing adventures and magical characters. Spider Suit Boy likes them best when something scary happens!

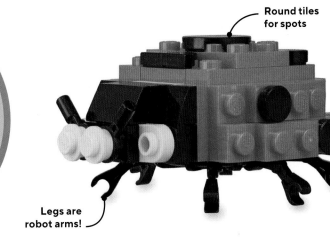

Round tiles for spots

Legs are robot arms!

Plates with clips make great spider legs

Will you give your spider teeth?

BUILD IT!

Build some LEGO creepy crawlies of your own—and make these characters the stars of your stories! Look for pieces that would work for legs, tentacles, antennae, and other cool body parts. Your creatures don't need to look realistic. The stranger they are, the more interesting your stories will be!

TOP TIP!

Use all kinds of colors and let your imagination run wild.

Make a snail's shell with curved bricks

Cones are handy for eye stalks

WHEELCHAIR RACER

There is no stopping Wheelchair Racer when he is on a roll. Sprints, relays, marathons... he has won them all—and he has the medals to prove it. After a race, he likes to wind down by playing games on his video console. Racing games, obviously.

What did one tire say to the other?

Wheel get through this!

MINI FACTS

LIKES Going faster, and faster, and faster...

DISLIKES Punctures

OFTEN SAYS "Wanna race?"

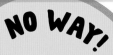

NO WAY!

Wheelchair racers compete in specialized wheelchairs. The world's fastest wheelchair racers can reach speeds of 18.6 miles (30 kilometers) per hour or more!

RACE TO THE TOP

Do you have what it takes to get to the top? In this speed-building game, the player who builds the tallest tower in 30 seconds wins. It sounds easy, but be careful—the taller your tower gets, the more likely it is to wobble and fall. If it does, you will have to start again, and build even faster to try to catch up.

HOW TO PLAY

1 Give each player a pile of bricks of exactly the same number and size.

2 Set a timer for 30 seconds. Everyone now starts building a tower with their bricks. When the 30 seconds is up, stop building.

3 Wait another 10 seconds, just in case someone's tower is on the point of collapsing. The winner is the player with the tallest tower that remains standing.

Well done, Gorilla Suit Guy!

To make the game even trickier, ask everyone to add a minifigure at the end!

Build a wide base for better stability

WANNA RACE?

A race? Er... not today! Race Car Guy knows he is nowhere near as fast as Wheelchair Racer. He would be left way behind in a cloud of dust. And who wants dust on their nice clean car costume?

CENTAUR WARRIOR

What do you call a horse that lives next door?

*A **neiiiigh**-bor!*

This master archer has the head and torso of a Minifigure and the legs and body of a horse. Centaur Warrior shoots apples for target practice—and then eats the apples for a snack. She doesn't mind the holes!

MINI FACTS

LIKES Archery and reading fantasy stories

DISLIKES Losing at archery tournaments

BEST ADVICE Always keep your eyes on the prize

HORSING AROUND

Cowboy Costume Guy thinks it would be fun to have horse legs like Centaur Warrior. He likes to think he looks a bit like her in his galloping horse costume.

FRIGHT KNIGHT

Fright Knight has a very important job. He is in charge of all scary noises at Night Lord's castle. Strange moans, clanking chains, and sudden bangs are all his speciality.

NO WAY!

Castles were built to impress and frighten the world for hundreds of years. 10,000 castles were built in Spain through the ages. Around 2,500 of them have survived.

MINI FACTS

LIKES Perfecting new creepy sounds

DISLIKES Being told he is not as scary as his cousin, the Frightening Knight

OFTEN FOUND Volunteering at a stray bats' home

What do ghosts put in their hair?

Scare spray!

KNIGHT TERROR

Tournament Knight ran very fast when he heard a mysterious sound at Night Lord's castle. But then he realized it was just his old friend Fright Knight.

BEAR COSTUME GUY

How do you wrap a cloud?

With a rain-bow!

Bear Costume Guy adds color to every Minifigure's day. He spreads love, laughter, and kindness wherever he goes. He feels very lucky that he found this awesome bear suit deep in a crystal cave in the mountains.

NO WAY!

Rainbows form when sunlight bounces off raindrops and splits into different colors. Although they look arc-shaped, rainbows are full circles! You just can't usually see the bottom.

 **MINI FACTS**

LIKES Handing out rainbows and hearts to everyone he meets

DISLIKES Nothing—he tries to see the good in everything

OFTEN FOUND Cheering up any friends who are sad

Angle the plates to make a quarter-circle shape

Gold coins are 1x1 round plates

BUILD IT!

Bear Costume Guy adores building LEGO rainbows. Try making one of your own. You could stack bricks into a staircase shape. Or place plates onto a baseplate for a flat LEGO rainbow picture. Why not add eyes to make it extra magical? You could even add a pot of gold at the end!

1x1 plate

Eyes attach to bricks with side studs

Most of this rainbow is made from 2x2 bricks

White bricks are clouds

EPIC QUEST

Unicorn Guy and Bear Costume Guy turn everyday walks into magical adventures. All it takes is some imagination. A sprinkle of glitter helps, too!

83

COWBOY COSTUME GUY

Giddy-up! A simple cowboy costume is not enough for this fun-loving Minifigure. His outfit makes him look like he is riding a horse, too! Everyone loves having this funny and friendly Minifigure around.

Why did the horse cross the road?

Because somebody shouted "hay"!

NO WAY!

Within one hour of being born, a foal can stand up on its own—on four very wobbly legs. It takes around four years for horses to become fully grown.

MINI FACTS

LIKES Galloping off into the sunset

DISLIKES Taking his costume off to go to the toilet

KNOWS A stable-load of horse jokes

MINIFIGURE MAYHEM

Saddle up for a game of Minifigure charades. Have you ever wondered what it is like to be your favorite character? Well, now is your chance! You could trot around as Cowboy Costume Guy. Or belt out a song as Cabaret Singer—in silence, of course!

HOW TO PLAY

1 Put some Minifigures into a bag or box for players to choose from.

2 Pick a Minifigure (making sure nobody sees who you have picked) and act out the character by miming. You can't use any words!

3 The other players have one minute to guess the Minifigure correctly. Take it in turns to play.

HOWDY, PARTNER!

Nobody laughs at Cowboy Costume Guy's jokes more than Horse and Groom. They adore him trotting by for a visit.

85

LLAMA COSTUME GIRL

What do llamas say when someone thanks them?

No prob-llama!

Llama Costume Girl spends her days caring for llamas on her ranch. She wears a llama costume to put her furry friends at ease. Well, she also wears it because it is super comfortable and she looks llama-mazing in it! Don't you agree?

 **MINI FACTS**

LIKES Reading to her llamas

DISLIKES Collecting llama poop to use as fertilizer

NEVER Mixes up her llamas. She always remembers every one of their names

COSTUMED CHUMS

Elephant Costume Girl was having such a fun day at her pal's ranch. That is until she spotted a mouse – eeek!

FIGURE SKATING CHAMPION

Watch this dazzling Minifigure toe loop and flip across the ice rink. If you are lucky, he may even cook up a meal for you afterward. Those ice skates come in very handy for chopping vegetables.

MINI FACTS

LIKES Winning trophies and medals

DISLIKES His hair falling out of place

FAVORITE JUMP The quadruple axel—he studies and practices it every single day

Why did the figure skater forget to turn up to practice?

It just slipped his mind!

ICE TO SEE YOU

Figure Skating Champion was surprised to have a visitor when he was practicing in the wild. Paddle Surfer had taken a few wrong turns!

MINIFIGURE CHAMPS

These sporty Minifigures don't stay still for long. Whether they are on land, sea, or ice, they love being active. Some are serious athletes while others just enjoy their hobbies, but they all have fun. Which sport would you like to try?

One quadruple axel coming up! I just need some ice...

Surf's up!

PROGRAMMER

Programmer is always finding ways to have fun with technology. She built a pet robot—Built Utility Buddy, or B.U.B. for short. Do you want to see B.U.B.'s new trick? Just wait a few minutes while Programmer writes some code.

How do you make a robot angry?

Push its buttons!

01001100
01000101
01000111
01001111

LEVEL UP

These best friends are not just whizzes at playing computer games, they design them, too. Video Game Champ's latest idea is a shark game called Big Byte.

SPIDER SUIT BOY

BOO! Minifigures should watch out for Spider Suit Boy. This so-called scary Minifigure likes to jump out and surprise them with his spooky handmade costumes.

NO WAY!

The world's biggest spider is the Goliath birdeater. It is 12 inches (30.5 centimeters) long. The world's smallest spiders are around 0.015 of an inch (0.4 millimeters) long.

MINI FACTS

LIKES Having several pairs of eyes

DISLIKES Losing a spider leg

PRETENDS To not like parties, but he always joins in eventually

SPIDER LULLABY

Spider Suit Boy likes to act like he is unfriendly, but he is actually very kind. He sings "Itsy Bitsy Spider" to Pajama Girl when she struggles to sleep.

What do spiders like to do on computers?

*Make **web**sites!*

DRAGON SUIT GUY

Dragon Suit Guy likes his food hot, hot, hot. He piles on the chili peppers at every meal—including his breakfast cereal! Luckily, Dragon Suit Guy isn't at all hot-tempered. The fieriest thing to come out of his mouth is an occasional chili-powered burp.

NO WAY!

Legends about dragons come from all over the world, but only three countries have a dragon on their flag. They are Wales, Malta, and Bhutan.

What does a dragon like to eat at a restaurant?

Hot wings!

MINI FACTS

LIKES Perfecting his homemade hot sauce recipe

DISLIKES Bland food

OFTEN SEEN Trying to spice up his pals' lives by gifting them bottles of hot sauce

White round plates for eyes and teeth

Quarter-circle pieces

BUILD IT!

Check out medieval or Chinese art for pictures of dragons to inspire your LEGO® builds. These styles of dragons look very different from each other. You could also take inspiration from a favorite book, movie, TV show, or video game. Or if research sounds like a drag, simply use your own imagination.

TOP TIP!

Use axles or ball joints to attach wings that can really flap.

Chameleonlike eyes

Wing with pin hole and axle

Fiery tongue

PROTECTING THE PLANET

Racoon Costume Fan wants to make the world a greener place. She has taught Dragon Suit Guy to recycle hot-sauce bottles instead of throwing them in the trash.

SHIPWRECK SURVIVOR

Sea, sand, and endless sunshine—life is one long holiday for Shipwreck Survivor. He is stranded on a paradise island and has no plans to escape. That message in a bottle? He isn't asking for help. He is just seeking a pen pal.

What happened when I tried to say the alphabet?

I got lost at "C"!

ISLAND GUEST

Pirate Girl often drops anchor to visit Shipwreck Survivor. After a chat on the beach they sit down to his famous home-cooked dish, "Coconut 50 ways."

MOUNTAIN BIKER

Mountain Biker gets her name from her mode of transportation, but you will never see her on a mountain. Or a hill. Pedaling along a nice flat river or canal path is much more her style. She gives the bumpier routes a flat "no."

How does a snowman get to work?

By icicle!

MINI FACTS

LIKES A smooth ride (and a refreshing smoothie at the end)

DISLIKES Getting all shaken up

DREAM To cycle along every river in the world, from A to Z

NO WAY!

In 1896, the US Army experimented with using mountain bikes instead of horses. There was a special unit called the 25th Infantry Bicycle Corps.

WHEELY GOOD PALS

The paths are quieter in the evenings. That is when Mountain Biker and Wheelchair Racer meet up for a friendly race or two.

LEGO BRICK SUIT GUY

What happened when I met LEGO Brick Suit Girl?

We just connected!

LEGO Brick Suit Guy takes life one brick at a time. Well, he has to, really. He is a Minifigure, so each brick is h-u-g-e to him! He loves party games, especially building ones where he can take charge. Bricks at the ready; one, two, three... build!

MINI FACTS

LIKES Following the step-by-step instructions

DISLIKES Losing the step-by-step instructions

OFTEN SAYS "LEGO bricks rock!"

NO WAY!

LEGO bricks have been to space! In 2011, astronauts on the International Space Station built a LEGO model of... the International Space Station.

CHOPSTICK CHALLENGE

Do you have a firm grip? Then try this brick-picking game. You have 30 seconds to pick up as many LEGO pieces as you can and move them to a new pile. The catch is you have to use chopsticks. If you drop a piece, it must go back on the original pile. No cheating!

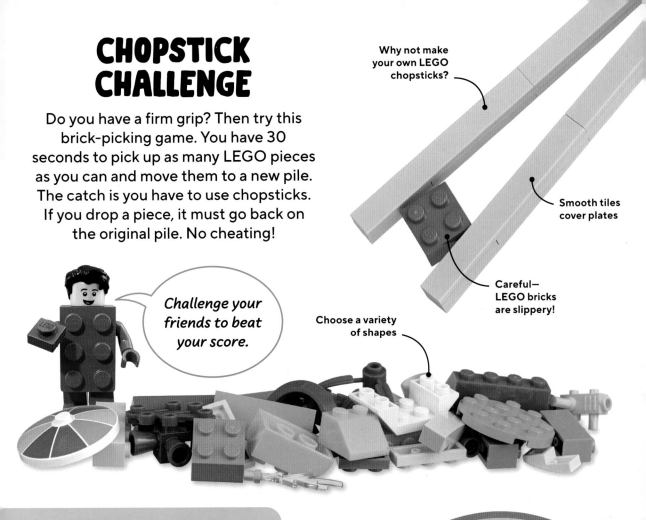

Why not make your own LEGO chopsticks?

Smooth tiles cover plates

Careful— LEGO bricks are slippery!

Challenge your friends to beat your score.

Choose a variety of shapes

A PERFECT MATCH

Some partygoers don't like meeting another guest in a similar outfit, but Brick Suit Guy and Brick Suit Girl didn't mind. It proved that they both had excellent taste.

HOW TO PLAY

1 Find some chopsticks—or build some with LEGO bricks! Make a pile of mixed LEGO elements.

2 Set a timer for 30 seconds. Now use the chopsticks to pick up pieces and make a new pile.

3 When the timer goes off, count the pieces in the new pile. Score one point for each piece.

PAJAMA GIRL

Pajama Girl loves getting into her soft, snuggly pajamas at night. But is she ready to sleep? Well, maybe in a minute. But first, she'd like another story. And another sip of water. And another blanket. And another carrot for her bunny...

MINI FACTS

LIKES Bunny rabbits

DISLIKES Coming to the last page in a book

OFTEN SAYS "Just one more bedtime story..."

What do you call a sleeping T. rex?

A dino*snore*!

TELL A BEDTIME STORY

Dream up a bedtime story, then use LEGO builds to tell it. Will the Shipwreck Survivor escape his desert island? Is the T. rex upset that Pajama Girl has woken him? How on earth will the Princess get out of that swamp? The ending is up to you.

Flagpole is bar and plate with clip

Tattered jeans

Hi, Mr. Rex. I like your striped pajamas!

Slopes for dino feet

Legs removed so Princess looks like she is sinking

DREAM TEAM

Every bedtime, Night Protector welcomes Pajama Girl to the world of dreams. This magical guardian always has a long wait. Pajama Girl does take her time nodding off!

MONKEY KING

He doesn't look it, but Monkey King is thousands of years old. He hatched from an egg, survived being buried in rock, and wields a staff that is heavier than an elephant. That's monkey magic!

MINI FACTS

LIKES Stealing peaches

DISLIKES Demons—he is always fighting them

SPECIAL TRICK Shrinking his staff down to tuck behind his ear

Which monkey floats in the sky?

A hot-air baboon!

HEAVY LIFTING

Monkey King offered to let his friend hold the magic staff. But Dragon Suit Guy couldn't even lift it. If only he were a magic dragon!

FIREWORK GUY

Hey, is it time to turn on the lights? You can count on Firework Guy to lead the countdown to anything. But there is no need to take cover when he explodes. All you'll get is a happy shout and a shower of confetti.

What happened when the firework took an exam?

He passed with flying colors!

 **MINI FACTS**

LIKES Loud noises

DISLIKES Going for a whole week without a party

OFTEN SAYS "5... 4... 3... 2... 1... BANG!"

SPARKLING MOVES

Firework Guy and Cactus Girl love to dance, especially at a fireworks display. What kind of music do they like? Rocket 'n' roll!

FLOWERPOT GIRL

What's my favorite kind of music?

Heavy petal!

Flowerpot Girl was once a shy little bud, but now she has blossomed into the star of every gathering. Naturally, garden parties are her favorite. She sometimes dances so hard she starts to wilt. But she soon perks up after a drink of water!

NO WAY!

Some flowering plants don't need soil to grow in. Orchids can grow by clinging to trees. Their roots get nutrients from the air instead of earth.

 MINI FACTS

LIKES Sunshine, fresh air, and friends

DISLIKES When bees think she is a real flower

FAVORITE SPOT In the sun with a bit of shade

Petals clip onto bars

TOP TIP!

Use clip-and-bar connections to add petals that can be angled.

Round tiles look like puffy petals

BUILD IT!

Use your LEGO bricks to build a garden bursting with blooms, from golden daffodils to plump poppies. Base your flowers on real plants, or let your imagination run wild. You could set the flowers on brown tiles to represent patches of soil. Flowerpot Girl thinks they might look even better in colorful flowerpots, though.

Dish with sprinkles

Petals attach to octagonal ring

Plant leaf

Curved slopes for rounded pot

SOWING THE SEEDS OF FRIENDSHIP

The first time Flowerpot Girl met Brick Costume Guy, she admired his suit. It was the perfect shade of leaf green! Now they have a flourishing friendship.

TOURNAMENT KNIGHT

Tournament Knight is a bit tired of his day job. It is an endless round of jousts and dragon hunts. Frankly, he would rather be playing "Staplers and Spreadsheets," a thrilling, multi-level fantasy game based on office life. Yield, printer!

> How long does a jousting match last?
>
> Until **knight**-fall!

NO WAY!

The aim in a joust is to knock another knight off their horse. In medieval times, some knights bolted their armor to the saddle so they would stay on. Such cheats!

MINI FACTS

LIKES Role-playing games with Viking and Pirate Queen

DISLIKES Crawling through dungeons. So mucky!

BATTLE CRY "Yield, varlet!"

CASTLE QUEST

Most knights would prefer a large, fancy castle, but small and simple wins the day in this game. The victor is the player who builds a castle using the fewest elements. Remember, it has to be something Tournament Knight would recognize, so think about what features most shout "castle" to you.

HOW TO PLAY

1 Decide on a few features every build must include, such as a tower, a drawbridge, a grassy surround, and perhaps a moat.

2 Players build a castle using the smallest number of pieces possible.

3 The player whose castle has the fewest pieces wins. If you can't agree whether it's recognizable, ask someone not playing what they think the build is.

Tower topped by slope bricks

Stack bricks to create turrets

Slope as lowered drawbridge

Pyramid roof

Trees in castle grounds

Green plate looks like grass patch

MEDIEVAL MUSIC LOVERS

Troubadour is happy to take song requests from Tournament Knight. Happy, but not exactly tuneful. What's his most requested song? "Knight Fever"!

TO THE RESCUE!

Hooray! These brave and hardworking Minifigures are here to save the day. Whether they are rescuing animals, patrolling the streets, or guarding mysterious worlds, they've all got your back. Which Minifigure hero would you most like to be?

Where's the fire?

I hope this quest doesn't drag on. It's nearly dinner time!

POLICE

This way to the beach!
I will do everything to protect my frozen realm. There's snow place like home!
Did you call me? I usually nap during the day.

CHILI COSTUME FAN

Why did the pepper put on a sweater?

Because it was a little chili!

No chili is too hot for this Minifigure! She enjoys testing herself by eating the spiciest chili peppers she can find. She does get a bit sweaty sometimes, but she likes to blame it on the warm costume. It is definitely NOT the chilies!

MINI FACTS

LIKES Chili peppers!

DISLIKES Mild chili peppers. What is the point?

FAVORITE DRINK A cooling glass of ice-cold milk (but don't tell anyone!)

TOP THAT!

Chili Costume Fan thinks pizzas topped with plenty of chili and spicy sausage are the best. Pizza Costume Guy thinks all pizzas are delicious, whatever the topping!

'80s MUSICIAN

This totally rad Minifigure has been rocking out with his keytar ever since he bought one in the 1980s. You will find him busking at the shopping mall, playing songs from his favorite classic movies. Gnarly!

NO WAY!

The keytar is shaped like a guitar, but it is really just a lightweight keyboard. It was popular in the 1980s, and it allowed keyboard players to take center stage. Awesome!

MINI FACTS

LIKES Watching 1980s romantic comedies

DISLIKES Forgetting the power cable for his keytar

FAVORITE BAND Brickwave

DAZZLING DUET

Violin Kid and '80s Musician have different musical backgrounds. But they are both equally passionate about music. Rock on!

Where did the music teacher leave his keys?

In the piano!

SPACE CREATURE

Space Creature once lived a life of crime, stealing from spaceships all over the galaxy. It took a spell in Space Jail to turn their life around. Now, they are a loyal member of the Space Police!

Where does an alien park its ship?

At a parking meteor!

MINI FACTS

LIKES A thrilling space chase

DISLIKES The food rations in Space Jail. Yuck!

OFTEN SAYS "Redael ruoy ot em ekat!"

STELLAR FRIENDSHIP

Space Creature has abandoned their criminal life, but not their criminal friends. Shhh... don't tell the Space Police that Space Creature has met up with Alien, the crystal thief!

Movable antenna

Steering wheel nose

Does this alien swivel its ears to communicate?

Purple leaf pieces for alien feet

Arms are plant tendrils

BUILD IT!

Nobody has seen all the aliens in the galaxy—not even Space Creature. That means you can make your LEGO® aliens look however you want, so let your imagination loose. Tentacles instead of arms? Yes! A nose that spins? Of course! Suction-cup feet? Perfect!

Big eyes look out for space crystals

TOP TIP!

Make a mob of matching aliens and stage an Earth invasion!

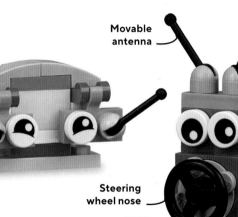

111

PIZZA COSTUME GUY

Pizza Costume Guy has a job that is hard to top. He is a pizza restaurant's mascot, hired to entice hungry passers-by into a fragrant world of cheesy goodness. For a pizza fan like him, there is no better way to earn a crust.

Did you hear the latest pizza joke?

Never mind—it's too cheesy!

NO WAY!

The world record for the fastest time to eat a 12-inch pizza (with a knife and fork) is 23.62 seconds. But Pizza Costume Guy thinks it's best to savor pizza!

PIZZA

1$

1$

MINI FACTS

LIKES Extra toppings

DISLIKES Standing around getting cold

FAVORITE FOOD What a silly question!

Green flower elements as peppers

Crust made from curved tiles

HOW TO PLAY

1 Build each chef a pizza base. Then gather a pile of LEGO food pieces and other small elements.

2 Decide on one player to be the chef and another to be the customer for each round.

3 Set a timer for 20 seconds. The customer calls out toppings and the chef races to make a pizza that looks like the order. The chef who makes the most perfect pizza wins.

FAST DELIVERY

How long would it take to load a LEGO pizza base with a tumble of toppings? You are aiming for 20 seconds in this LEGO pizza-making competition! The customer gets to choose the toppings, so look sharp, chef. You don't want your pizza to be sent back.

Round corner is pizza base

Pineapple chunk

LET'S PEA FRIENDS

Peapod Costume Girl has made friends with Pizza Costume Guy. She encourages him to use lots of <u>fresh vegetables</u> on his pizzas.

Hot dog element

RACOON COSTUME FAN

Who is that rifling through the trash cans? Is it an animal hunting for scraps? No, it is Racoon Costume Fan looking for trash to recycle. This nature lover is glad to have a chance to bring about a greener future. She is not about to throw it away!

> *What do you call a group of baby trash cans?*
>
> *A litter!*

MINI FACTS

LIKES Persuading pals to start recycling

DISLIKES Waste

TOP TIP Squash plastic bottles before recycling—it saves space

FURRY FRIENDS

Cat Costume Girl was happy to go recycling with her pal, until she realized she would have to get up at 4am. That is her catnap time!

SNOW GUARDIAN

Defending the innocent (and the chilly) is the job of Snow Guardian. You will always get a warm welcome from this cool guy. But wrap up well if you visit him—he lives in a frozen castle in the northern realms, where icy winds never stop blowing. Brrr!

NO WAY!

Snow is frozen water. So why is it white? It is because of the way light bounces off the many sides of the ice crystals that make up snowflakes.

What does a snowman have on his bed?

A blanket of snow!

COOL COMPANY

Figure Skating Champion has won a gold cup. He is celebrating by sharing a cold drink with his buddy Snow Guardian. Served in the trophy, of course.

PADDLE SURFER

As soon as the sun is up, Paddle Surfer is, too. She can't wait to get out on the waves, searching for distant lagoons and hidden coves. At low tide, Paddle Surfer is a volunteer litter-picker, helped by her dolphin pal, Eco. They are a tidy twosome!

NO WAY!

Imagine doing yoga while balancing on a paddle board! Amazingly, SUP (stand-up paddle board) yoga is a real activity. It's best not to try it if the water is choppy!

MINI FACTS

LIKES Locating an unexplored lagoon

DISLIKES Discarded bottles, cans, and plastic bags

OFTEN SAYS "Surf's up!"

What did the sea say to the dolphin?

Nothing... it just waved!

Slopes are great for making tail fins

Curved arches form humps

Sea made of blue plates

BUILD IT!

Paddle Surfer hasn't yet spotted any mythical sea creatures on her travels. Why not build a friendly mermaid or merman for her to meet at sea? Or you could build a mysterious sea monster for her to discover, like this sea serpent. Will it be friendly, or looking for its lunch?

TOP TIP!

If you make the tail separately, it will look like it's poking out of the water.

Mermaids usually have long hair

Movable arms

Orange tail fin

THE COAST IS CLEAR

Sea Rescuer often helps Paddle Surfer to clear up litter along the coastline. They both know that as well as looking awful, it is a danger to wildlife, too.

LEGO BRICK SUIT GIRL

LEGO Brick Suit Girl relies on her imagination, not instructions. Her builds are unique, and often feature wild shapes and colors. She is always encouraging others to unleash their creativity, too. Why not give it a try?

Why did the LEGO brick cry?

It was feeling blue!

NO WAY!

If you had six 2x4 LEGO bricks, you could combine them in more than 915 million ways. LEGO Brick Suit Girl has probably tried them all!

MINI FACTS

LIKES Thinking outside the box

DISLIKES Too many rules and regulations

PROUDEST MOMENT Winning a LEGO building contest

ONE THING LEADS TO ANOTHER...

Creativity is catching! In this game, you and your friends join efforts to make weird, wild models. It's a timed game, so think quickly about imaginative ways to add pieces. Could those horns be arms? Could that sword be a tail?

HOW TO PLAY

1 Gather your friends around a pile of LEGO pieces. Set a timer for one minute. Everyone chooses 10 pieces and starts building.

2 After one minute, reset the timer. Players pass their model to the person on their left. Everyone adds another 10 pieces to the model in front of them.

3 Continue in rounds until everyone has added pieces to all the models. What surprising builds have you made?

The initial build is just a car

In round 2, horns have been added

Simple wheels

Antennae for ears

Tail is a golden sword

It has turned into a creature on wheels!

PARTY PARTNERS

LEGO Brick Suit Girl has partnered with Birthday Party Girl for a game. She can tell her new friend is going to be fun. Just look at that giant purple balloon!

Wolf car headlights

119

BEEKEEPER

Beekeeper once had an exciting job as a detective. Now that he has retired, his days are filled with a different kind of buzz. He raises bee colonies and collects their honey from hives built from LEGO bricks. Yes, life is sweet for Beekeeper.

NO WAY!

That container in Beekeeper's hand is a bee smoker. Puffing smoke into a hive makes the bees calm down, so they are much less likely to sting.

> Where do bees keep their savings?
>
> In a honey box!

MINI FACTS

LIKES Honey on his morning toast

DISLIKES Getting stung. There is always one bee that wants to play rough

OFTEN SAYS "Bzzz bzzz bzzz!"

BEE MY GUEST

Beekeeper invited Jungle Explorer to watch him at work. But he warned his friend to stand back. Harvesting honey can be a sticky business.

SPACE POLICE GUY

?

"Freeze, lawbreaker!" Space Police Guy is here to uphold Space Law. He is an ice-cool cop with a zero-tolerance policy. Don't let him catch you dropping litter in an asteroid field. For him, that's the start of a slippery slope to a criminal career.

MINI FACTS

LIKES Citizens who abide by Space Law

DISLIKES Crooks escaping

TRAINED AT A Futuron academy on the Ice Planet

Where do snowmen like to dance?

At a snow ball!

POLICE

CHILLING TOGETHER

When Space Police Guy is off duty, he visits Snow Guardian at his frozen castle. They enjoy a nice iced tea together.

BIRTHDAY PARTY BOY

Birthday Party Boy is always thrilled to be invited to any party or celebration. He met lots of famous LEGO Minifigures at his first-ever party. Everyone was so friendly! Now that he is famous himself, he always gives new Minifigures a warm welcome.

 **MINI FACTS**

LIKES Meeting his Minifigure heroes

DISLIKES When a party invite goes astray

PARTIES ATTENDED He lost count a long time ago

What kind of music does a party balloon dislike?

Pop music!

NO WAY!

The world record for the fastest time to create one balloon dog sculpture is six and a half seconds. Better start practicing!

GUESS WHO?

In this guessing game, you and your friends question a hidden Minifigure to discover their identity. Sounds easy? Not really, because you are limited to questions that can be answered "yes" or "no." The person who guesses the Minifigure wins the round and becomes the next chooser.

HOW TO PLAY

1 Find a box with a lid, or use your LEGO bricks to build one. It must be large enough to fit a Minifigure inside.

2 Decide on one person to be the chooser. Everyone else turns away while the chooser hides a Minifigure inside the box.

3 Players take turns to ask the chooser questions that can only be answered with "yes" or "no." The first person to guess correctly wins.

Do I have a furry tail?
Yes!

Do I swim in the sea?
No!

Am I a sports star?
No!

Do I play an instrument?
Yes!

BIRTHDAY BASH BUDDIES

Opening a prize or a present is fun! Birthday Party Boy likes to unwrap his carefully. His friend Piñata Boy prefers to bash his way in as fast as he can.

123

DK | Penguin Random House

Senior Editor Helen Murray
Senior US Editor Megan Douglass
Project Art Editor Jenny Edwards
Production Editor Siu Yin Chan
Production Controller Lloyd Robertson
Managing Editor Paula Regan
Managing Art Editor Jo Connor
Publishing Director Mark Searle

Models designed and created by
Jason Briscoe, Emily Corl, Nate Dias, Jessica Farrell,
Rod Gillies, Steve Guinness, Kevin Hall, Nina Koopman,
Barney Main, James McKeag, and Simon Pickard.

Dorling Kindersley would like to thank: Tess Howarth, Randi Sørensen,
Heidi K. Jensen, Paul Hansford, and Martin Leighton Lindhardt at the
LEGO Group; Gary Ombler for additional photography; Hannah Dolan
for proofreading.

First American Edition, 2022
Published in the United States by DK Publishing
1450 Broadway, Suite 801, New York, NY 10018

Manufactured by Dorling Kindersley, One Embassy Gardens, 8 Viaduct
Gardens, London SW11 7BW, under license from the LEGO Group.

Published in Great Britain by Dorling Kindersley Limited
A catalog record for this book
is available from the Library of Congress.
ISBN 978-0-7440-5464-4 (trade edition)
978-0-7440-5689-1 (library edition)

Printed and bound in China

For the curious

www.dk.com

www.LEGO.com

JUL 2022